THE GANG OF
WONDER
KIDS

THE GANG OF
WONDER
KIDS

SHETALL RAMSINGHANI

PARTRIDGE

A Penguin Random House Company

To order additional copies of this book, contact
Partridge India
000 800 10062 62
orders.india@partridgepublishing.com

www.partridgepublishing.com/india

Contents

I dedicate this book to my young friends:-

Naina Rao, Ujjwal Kansra, Utsav Kansra, Manas Dhingra, Sankalp Malhotra, Rohan and Vikram Jyot Singh

Thank you note

My heartfelt gratitude to all my readers, who without fail follow my blogs, buy my books and have courtesy to review it and recommend it further too.

I would also like to thank my publishing agency Partridge India and their hard working staff Nelson Cortez, Gemma Ramos & Thomas Mc. Kinley for helping me getting my books published and for their timely guidance and of course their participation in marketing my books.

After writing Love beyond veils (My first book of Poems) and The Golden Hour (Short stories) I was very contented. I had decided to continue blogging and a dream to write a book was somewhere over. As an old saying goes: - "When the student is ready, master appears". My thoughts might not be in sync with my contentment. I wanted to learn more and to explore more of what life is all about.

It was 14th June 2014, weekend had started. It was lazy late morning of Saturday, when a little boy of the age 10 knocked the door of my house. As I opened it, he asked me if he was welcome into my house. I was astound as I never had a visitor during the weekend and that too uninvited.

Nevertheless, I escorted him to my living room wondering why this young boy was at my door that too with such a serious face. I asked him if he would like to have something and he simple said no. He sat on the sofa and kept on looking at me with a smiling face, I too smiled back thinking what he's gonna say now.

He was quiet with a smiling face and there was a silence in the room someone had to break the ice so I started asking who he is and where he puts up.

You are Sheetal didi right?

Right. And you I asked?

I am Ujjwal; I stay at the end of this lane.

Nice to meet you Ujjwal.

You have a cute dog; I too have a dog at home. Can I play with him, said He.

I let Sultan (My furry friend) enter the living area and he started playing. For another 15 minutes he was playing with my puppy and then bid me bye.

That was quiet strange! I said to myself.

Same day in the evening, he came again and I called Sultan to play with him, to which he said no, I am not here to play with Sultan. I want to talk to you.

Me?

He nodded his head in yes and once again we sat as if some important business meeting was about to start or as if he has some million dollar proposal for me. Anyway I had to break the ice again by offering him some sweets. What do you want to talk about kid?

Ujjwal was bit hesitant but once he started talking there was no looking back. My interview begins with celebrity Ujjwal somewhat like this:-

So, you write books?

Yes

I know that you have published two books. I have seen that on internet.

I nodded and said Thanks.

Do you take money for writing books?

No, from whom do I take money from?

Then how do you write books

Ummm, I think and then I type sometimes I research and add on to my stories

No, What I mean is who asks you to write

No one

If someone asks you to write a book will you write?

Well, depends

Hummm now he took a pause.

Will you write a book for me?

I gave him a big smile and asked him what does he want me to write on?

He said anything for me

Okay, I will write.

He immediately got up saying I have to go now, please write a book for me.

I laughed and shared that incident with my family.

I slept over his thought

Next morning, he came and asked whether I have finished writing a book?

I laughed and explained to him that it takes time.

After this, this little boy came everyday asking me the same question.

Now something inside me was telling that he was serious, he actually wants a book, I guess none of my bosses has given me an ultimatum to write the way this 10 year old boy gave. To give a full stop to his thought, I wrote a story for him and blogged it as well, giving him the print out I thought the case was closed but I was wrong. He came the next day along with his friends and appreciated my effort in writing a story and said will this be in book?

My mouth was wide open, he actually wanted a book!

What do I write? Writing books for children is not that easy that too who are reaching their adolescent age, Moreover that is not my niche....rest was history.

One out of these wonder kids was Naina. The girl brought all the storybooks which had quizzes for kids, she even gave me her detective novels to read on...But, I hardly had time to read and write as I am a working girl. No wonder, I did take her help as far as the quizzes in this book are concerned.

Before writing a book I wanted to to spend time with these children to know them better. Every evening they would come and share how their day went by. I have lived and recalled every moment of my childhood with them. Whether it was crossing the road for the first time or eating out Momo's with friends for the first time. Writing poems or playing Name, place, animal thing on the last page of notebook.

I ended up recalling little Sheetal who I had left with my dear past somewhere.

To tell you the truth this book is a work of Nonfiction coated with fiction. Some incidents were actually lived by them, whether talking about the girls in the class, the nasty subjects, the fights, their high and lows in life; I have studied these kids carefully and came up with an idea to write a book on their own experiences in life.

Each story in this book ends with moral and I am sure kids would be happy to recognize themselves in the character and be a good human, spreading positivity to make this world a better place to live in.

Ujjwal's birthday is on 30th December. I am on my way to fulfill a promise to this young man and pray for him to be a good man in his life and make his parents proud of him.

To many Ujjwals in this world, this is my sincere effort in bringing light to your lives, to make you understand the value of being good to all in this life. I request all my young readers to follow the path of goodness and make this world a better place to live.

Lots of Love & Light
Shetall

Introduction

Virender being an Army man has always felt his first responsibility is to protect his country and the other one was his own family. He was blessed to be married with his childhood love Sheena who always supported Virender in ups and downs of his life. A true better half, love of his life and a kind of a wife any man can dream of.

Life is not easy and when it comes to the family of an Army man where discipline and responsibilities came first, where everything was planned in advance life sometimes was like a machine for young boys Utsav and Ujjwal. Ustav was 12 and Ujjwal was 10. Their father Virender was very strict with them though he used to meet them once in a month or sometimes in six months because of his postings. He kept his family with his parents back in Delhi.

Whenever he used to visit them he made sure that the boys learnt discipline in life and for that he used to prepare a big chart for boys that had time to eat, sleep, play, and study too.

Virender and Sheena were the most compatible couple, truly in love with each other wanted their kids to have the best in their lives, hence there was so many restrictions on the children.

Somehow, the boys used to shine their parents name with high grades. Their behavior was taken as kind of snooty by others army families in parties. They never used to talk much with other kids of army men. Always busy learning from the internet, playing quizzes or solving puzzles. They were mostly pampered by grandparents and often used to share their dreams and thoughts with them. Their life was moving like a machine for the family with monotonous daily routines and they were happy and satisfied the way it was.

Sheena many times used to miss her husband. One day happy news knocked the doors of Virender and Sheena's when Virender announced his promotion along with the transfer to another city.

This time Sheena convinced Virender that kids needed their father as the age was very tender and they were soon going to enter adolescent period. Sheena also told him about the change and the aggression boys were building in their nature which was not focused to the right direction.

How do you want me to take care of them all alone? Your parents are old now and the energy level which boys have it is sometimes difficult to handle the boys. I too miss you very much. What is wrong in us staying together argued Sheena with Virender

Sheena, my love I understand that, but do you think mummy and papa would agree to shift? I am happy to take all of you along with me if they agree to come along with us.

Come on Virender, I too want them to stay with us. I cannot leave them on their own at this age but we need you too. I want you to talk to mummy and papa the first thing in the morning said Sheena while switching off the night lamp and going off to sleep angrily.

Virender was quiet. Somewhere he knew that his parents won't leave this house but he had to take care of his family too. He could not just run away from his responsibilities. He slept while thinking about it.

This was not the first transfer which the couple had to face. However, for the kids, yes it was. Virender had been to different places and kept his family in Delhi with his parents but this time the situation was different. The kids were growing and his marital life was not getting enough of his attention.

Papa, are we traveling along with you this time? Asked Utsaav Papa, will granddad and grandmother stay with us there in Gujarat?

Kids had several questions on their minds and so did the old parents. He never thought that this happy news would turn into a big burden.

Virender: Papa, since kids are growing up, we understand that they need both of us now and Sheena cannot handle them alone. I have been allotted a house in Army Cantt, we all can shift there and….

Before he could complete his sentence Virender's mother intervened, I am not leaving this house. I came as a bride in this house and now I am old. My body will only leave this house. We are not traveling with you anywhere.

Virender was quiet. His father patted his back and said we are old now. Boys are growing too its time that you take care of them. We will take care of ourselves don't worry.

Virender did not say a word and left his parents room with a sad heart.

He thought about it day and night. He was worried about his old parents. They refused to travel out of Delhi at this age. Sheena was worried about the boys getting less time with father and her time with her husband.

Virender parents were witnessing his distress but then they wanted Virender to take a decision

The family went through many sleepless nights before coming on to a conclusion.

Utsav and Ujjwal used to sleep with their grandparents. The fear of leaving their grandparents bought tears in their eyes.

Granny, how will we stay without you? What will happen now? Asked Ujjwal

The old lady smiled and said don't you worry. God's plans are perfect for each of us.

Utsav questioned what do you mean granny?

Let me tell you a story, once there was a young boy, he used to stay away from his parents. He loved his parents very much but then he was grown up man and now it was his time to earn money for his family and he was supposed to learn new ways of living his own life too. He applied for jobs and got the job outside his state and left his house only to start living in a different place.

For first few days he used to miss his parents very much and used to call them in morning, afternoon and also in evening to check their well beings. But then soon opportunities and work around took toll on him and his calls were reduced from everyday to once in a week but everyday he used to pray for the happiness of his parents. His mother made him a god follower and his trust in God was firm.

His parents felt bad but understood that he had a life to live. His mother everyday used to pray for the well being and prosperity of her son.

One morning the boy woke up late. He realized he was late for work so he rushed and got ready in a hurry. Driving his car he had many negative thoughts. He was thinking how his boss would be mad at him.

He started thinking like you Ujjwal what will happen now? But he prayed to God and asked for his help.

He met many traffic jams and red lights. He continued praying and then all of sudden his car refused to start. He prayed, "Please God let my car start soon or I will be fired from my Job."

Finally the car revved into motion and he reached his office.

Then during lunch hour, his sandwich was a Non- Veg sandwich, which he could not eat and he had to wait in line all over again to order a veg one.

He thought to himself: "If this day could get any worse"

In the evening, while returning from office, he got a call but before he could answer his phone's battery died.

He shook his head and said "Why God? Nothing went right today... Why God? Why did you do that?"

What will happen tomorrow? Just like Ujjwal asked. Boys giggled.

Then what happened granny asked little Ujjwal

Granny looked at her husband and smiled

The grand father said then let me tell you what happened.

Then the young boy slept and had a dream of a white luminous angelic figure.

The angelic figure said," My son, I am your guardian angel. This morning I sent one of my angels to battle the death angel to protect you. I let you sleep till late. Your car didn't start because there was a drunken driver on your route who would have hit you if you were on the road. The first person who made your sandwich today was sick and I didn't wanted you to catch what they had. I knew you couldn't afford to miss work. Your phone went dead because the person who was calling was going to give false witness about what you must have said on that call. I didn't let you talk to him so you would be covered.

Your parents pray for your well being everyday and they want you to prosper hence God set up everything in a way that everyone's prayers be heard today. Don't worry about tomorrow be thankful for today and yes don't forget to call your parents in the morning to thank them as their prayers played a big role in saving your life today.

The young boy woke up from the dream and realized that angel actually visited him and he thanked God and his guardian angel for saving his life and job today and called his parents first thing in the morning.

The phone was answered by his father and when he recited the whole incident to them over the phone, his father said never doubt God's plan for you as he has much better plans than you can even think off.

Utsav hugged his grandfather tight and said I will pray daily from now on for everyone and Ujjwal seconded Utsav's thought and hugged their grandparents and slept.

Virender and Sheena were too listening to this story while standing outside the room and smiled and hugged each other and went to sleep.

Next morning around 6 am Virender's sister Radha called up informing him that she is shifting back to India from London as her husband has resigned from the job. She informed that she would be reaching Delhi tomorrow.

This brought a big smile on his face and he said we would be waiting for them.

Since finding house was not easy in Delhi, Sheena and Virender decided to give this house to his sister till they would stay in Gujarat.

Things were decided and Radha was happy to accept the offer too and was more than happy to keep the parents with her.

While, the brother and sister were deciding on parents, the turmoil into old parent's heart of parting away from grand children went unnoticed.

On the day, they were leaving, Utsav's grandfather gave him a dairy and said whenever you miss us or feel no one can understand your thoughts just write it down in this diary. And when your diary is full, send it to this old man to read. They all cried and Utsav promised his grandfather that he would write his diary everyday and Ujjwal promised his grandmother that he would always follow God's plan.

Virender along with his family left for Gujarat happily whereas Radha and her husband along with their toddler took over there house and promised to take care of the old parents.

An Unforgettable Birthday

U pon reaching Gujarat they were amazed to witness the beauty of Gujarat. Virender along with his family was settling down in Kutch.

Virender took kids to watch the Rann of Kutch were the symphony of salt and stones cuddled on one side by the sea and the other by desert. The boys were amazed to witness such a beauty.

Utsav who was good at googling the history of a place and told the family that he read about the Rann of Kutch before coming. He told them that a salt marsh, bendecks the western tip of Gujarat with its surreal charm.

Ujjwal questioned what is salt marsh papa?
Where Virender smiled and told him that the name which springs from the inherent geographical features of this lad, latterly means Salt Marsh or salty desert of Kutch.

Kutch is the district of which this region is a part.

Yes Ujjwal, do you know this seasonally marshy land covers a region of more than 10,000 square kilometers and is divided into little Rann of Kutch and the great Rann of Kutch said Utsav

Ujjwal's mouth was wide opened as he could not understand anything and innocently replied NO.
That made everyone laugh.

It was night and Utsav was surfing internet for the major attraction of Kutch when Sheena his mother entered there room and asked them to sleep at once.

The young boys missed their story time with granddad and sometimes by grandmother.

Sheena noticed their agony of parting away from their grand parents and tried her best to compensate that time by reciting fairy tales to them now and then.

She started by telling them a tale.

Once upon a time, little Utsav along with his younger brother went to spend a weekend with their grandparents.

They were happily watching discovery channel at night when a thunderstorm broke out and the electricity supply was cut off. Their little flat plunged into darkness.

They were scared. Their granny told them to go off to sleep and left them into the room and went to sleep in her room.

It is so dark and I am afraid said Ujjwal to his brother Utsav.

Utsav was fearless and he always used to take care of his younger brother.

He smiled and got out of the bed and opened the curtains of the bedroom window. Both of them caught a glimpse of the moon in the sky.

Soon grand father came in to check on them and saw them watching moon. He said "Our lights may be off" but you can see God's light is on.

They both turned back and saw their grandfather smiling.

Utsav while hugging his grandfather asked "is the moon God's own light"?

Of course it is! My child

Ujjwal asked "Won't God put out off his light and go to sleep?"

No son smiled the grandfather. "God never goes to sleep."

In this simple and beautiful faith, kids said "Well as long as God is awake we are not afraid!

The grandfather smiled and Ujjwal and Utsav hopped into their beds to sleep.

The fear of darkness had gone.

Wow mother you too know how to tell stories. Sheena smiled and kissed Utsav and Ujjwal's forehead and bid them Goodnight and the kids slept very well

Slowly, the time shifted and it was already the end of February. The school was about to begin. The new session in the school was to be started soon in March. Thankfully, the admissions had been done and the kids were excited to experience their new school.

Life was once again on the trail. As March approached, new session started. They met new friends and new enemies too in the class.

Utsav and Ujjwal were more than brothers. They were best friend of each other and they had succeeded in making many common friends. However the only girl in their class was the granddaughter of the General. She was Naina. She was detested by both the boys for no reason. They both used to bully her a lot and Naina in return used to hit them hard.

Once out of the blue Utsav questioned Naina's intelligence by asking her questions among all of the friends

He asked do you know the long walk to freedom was whose autobiography?

To which Naina was quick to reply ha I am younger to you but I know it is Nelson Mandela

Ujjwal said okay we both are in same class then tell me how many rings are on the Olympic flag?

Naina was quick to reply Five

Both the brothers looked at each other. Naina looking at them said now it's my turn.

Okay go ahead said Utsav

If I have it, I don't share it. If I share it, I don't have it what is it?

Since Utsav was fast at surfing net from his phone he searched the answer immediately saying ha! it is very simple it is a Secret.

I saw you were surfing net on your phone. Answer on your own

Intelligent boy said I am doing that, I am answering on my own from my mouth can't you see and all of the kids started laughing.

Naina shrugged her shoulders and looked at Ujjwal

Tell me the full name of Barbie doll.

I don't play with Barbie dolls but I know her full name. It is Barbara Millicent Roberts.

The fight between them continued and they kept on showing each other the level of knowledge and intelligence they held.

Four months had passed. It was June Utsav's birthday. He was approaching teen age this month. The party, venue everything was planned in advance.

The summer holidays had started. Thinking now they were young enough to travel on their own, the boys along with friends decided to Dholavira.

Utsav to his mom on his birthday: Mummy, I want to go to Dholavira along with my friends.

Sheena: No, You will not go there, there have been cases of missing children.

Utsav did not heed up to his mother's advice and deemed that he was old enough to make his decision and without informing left the house along with his younger brother Ujjwal.

Dholavira, an archeological site in Kutch district, also known as kotada timba contains ruins of the ancient Harrappan city in the Indus Valley civilization. It dates back to 2900 BC and is also known for exceptional town planning and engineering.

That was their first step out without their parent's approval. They were not aware of what they were going to face next.

Since Naina was the only girl in the group she forced herself on them and went along.

The place fascinated kids and they decided to play around. As they were playing they did not notice dawn striking and all of a sudden they heard the sound of someone crying.

Everyone looked around but they could not spot anyone except them and it was 7 already. The place was desolated. The sound kept on bothering them and all of them took courage to move ahead to see who it was?

Naina, saw an old woman sitting far away down the wall. She immediately called everyone.

Kids were scared but they managed to reach out to her

Hello Aunty can we help? The woman stopped sobbing and looked at them and said no you cannot leave me alone and started looking here and there.

Utsav and Ujjwal along with Sankalp, Manas, Manit and Naina looked at each other and asked her one more time.

This time she told them that her daughter was lost. She was 12 years of age and was playing here only and now she cannot trace her.

Manas were scared and Ujjwal immediately said to Utsav brother I am 11.

Utsav could sense the fear of his brother but asked him to calm down.

Shh said Utsav the bravest among all or at least at that time he could show that. After all it's his birthday today and he is a teenager now. He said can we help you out.

Please tell us where was she and we would try find her

The lady pointed out towards north direction.

Naina: Look I think we should leave this place now, our parents must be worried

Manas intervened and repeated what Naina said.

The kids decided to run away instantly

While on their way back home they all were thinking of the incident and instantly Ujjwal said to them what if one of us was lost, would be still be going home?

They all were quiet and looked at each other.

Sankalp: but I am scared, it is almost 8 pm, my mommy will get angry

Everyone said so would be ours but we are kids of fighters and we must go back, they all nodded in agreement and decided to go back.

They heard the voice of the crying woman again and went back apologizing. Sankalp slipped and lost his watch as he fell.

The lady witnessed that and took his watch in her hands and gave it to him.

Thanks aunty said Sankalp.

Utsav and Naina came forward and said we would help you find your daughter.

They all joined hands and started moving towards north direction.

It was dark and they could hear unusual sounds. Naina immediately asked everyone to wait.

What happened asked Ujjwal

We do not know the girl's name how will we call her?

Oh yes said Ujjwal while scratching his head
See I told you I am more intelligent then you said Naina

Shut up this is not intelligence

We all were together; if you would be intelligent you could have asked the name and then move forward.

Witnessing Naina and Ujjwal fighting again, Utsav being the eldest intervened and asked them to shut up. He said, look we are far more ahead, it would be stupidity if we go back we can call out by shouting "is someone around".

Everyone nodded in agreement and they moved forward. They saw a cave and everyone entered that cave thinking that the girl would be there.

To their surprise they ended up entering into a forest. They were amazed but decided to move forward.

Sankalp looked at his watch again as the watch had titanium it could easily tell time in the dark too. He noticed it was five minutes to 8. He calmed down and moved forward.

All of a sudden, Manas leaned himself to a tree. Naina saw this and immediately shouted careful Manas.

Manas got scared and immediately stood up straight asking what had happened?

This is tree resin which has been fossilized. It is known as amber, it sometimes contain plant material or small animals which are trapped inside.

Oh my god, I too have read about this in my textbook but I did not notice thank you Naina.

Naina smiled and one more time they all together went forward.

As they all were moving forward shouting anyone around? Anyone lost?

Nobody reverted back but then Ujjwal immediately pushed Utsav harder, what you are doing Ujjwal I am your brother said Utsav while getting irked from his behaviour.

Brother you were about to put your foot on Poison Ivy, I saved you.

Poison Ivy?

Yes. Before Ujjwal could complete Sankalp said yes I have too read about it, isn't it a plant which produces skin irritant?

Manas answered yes. It is called urushiol. Touching poison ivy causes an allergic reaction usually in the form of an itchy rash on the skin.

While everyone was discussing Poison Ivy, Sankalp once again looked at his watch and noticed that time had stopped. It was still 5 minutes to 8 pm. That made his heart beat run fast and he informed his friends that something was wrong with this place and all must go back.

What made you think so Sankalp asked little Manit.

Can't you see time has stopped all of sudden?

The cell must be weak

No, I just bought that. It is brand new.

None of them agreed with him and he started running backwards. Everyone tried to stop him but he did not listen to anyone and soon they all could not hear his foot steps. That made everyone scared and they started walking backwards.

As they walked with their heart running fast and shivering voice they called up for Sankalp but no one replied.

I think we all must go back and inform our parents about this incident said Naina one more time.

They all decided to run back from where they came. Unfortunately all of them lost their way and fell into a big deep pit.

They stayed there for long crying for help but no one helped them. Suddenly they saw a girl hiding herself on the side.

Hello, who are you? Asked Ujjwal.

Utsav looked at her as it was dark they thought she must be some witch as they all hugged each other and moved backwards they all fell while putting their feet backwards as Sankalp was already lying over there unconscious.

What is happening where are we? Asked Ujjwal crying

The girl stood up and broke her silence asking if other kids were around. It was very dark and instead of looking at each other they touched each other's hand and asked who are you?

I have lost my way. I was here with my parents and my ball went into the cave. My mother asked me to come back but I did not listen to her and moved forward and landed myself into this big deep hole.

They all took a breath and told her we came here searching for you only, your mother was sitting outside and crying.

Ujjwal said crying our mommy also told us not to go anywhere alone and here we are looking for you.

Naina consoled Ujjwal by patting his back. Everyone was quite worried with what would happen next?

Ujjwal was missing his grandmother and the last story he heard from her.

Manas being the fat boy broke his silence and said he was hungry.

There were many pats on his back by his friends which asked him to be quite.

Manit was the youngest among them. He asked all of them while crying what will happen now? Will witch come and eat us?

Utsav said no Manit Witches are in fairytales only. There are no witches in this real world and all of sudden they heard the sound of a wolf.

They all hugged each other and the girl came to their side and hugged Utsav.

Everyone started missing their parents and started crying but there was no help.

Ujjwal tried being strong and said remember the story which grandma had told us Utsav

Which story?

He started reciting the story to everyone and in the end said don't worry God has a plan for us too.

They all slept crying.

It was almost 10 pm since the kids had gone missing. Everyone was invited to the birthday party of Utsav. Sheena and Virender were worried along with other parents.

Sheena started panicking. Where are my kids? I hope all is well with them.

They said they would be going to Dholavira said one of the parent

Dholavira? I asked him not to go there said Sheena

Kids are growing up they don't listen said one of the parent while crying for his kid.

They immediately went and informed the Police. The police came into action immediately and started search operation for all the kids.

Meanwhile, the kids were confused scared and hungry inside that big hole.

The dawn broke and the first sunlight touched Naina's cheek. She woke everyone up instantly and saw the other girl's face.

She asked her name?

I am Naveli.

Naveli, help me wake everyone up? We need to move from here...

Naveli helped Naina and they all started looking around. Sankalp once again looked at his watch which was showing the same time and he started crying. He looked at Naveli and started cursing her. It is all because of you that we all are stuck here.

While Utsav was trying to calm everyone they all heard footsteps.

There were four men outside the hole laughing at them

Good we have enough kids now for our work said one of them while throwing ladders for them to climb.

As soon as all of them were out of hole, their eyes were closed by a cloth and hands were tied with a big rope they all were taken to a place where plenty of kids were already working.

The minute cloth was removed from their eyes they were stunned. The faces of the guys were hidden by a mask.

Who were they? What do they want? Asked Utsav from Sankalp

Manas pleaded them to leave him and his friends. A tight slap landed on his face that made everyone else scared.

They were immediately asked to start the work of digging.

But what are we digging for asked Ujjwal

The elder guy took his jaw in his hand tight and said treasure. Ancient treasure is lying beneath the ground. The moment your job is done you will be released.

They all together started digging along with other children. The guys didn't know that they were not ordinary kids they were kids of Army men.

The moment kids saw that only one man was left along with them, they immediately attacked on the head of that man and tried to run along with other kids. One of the kids told them that it is not easy to get out as he had also tried it earlier and the head of all the goons was just behind the front red door. Last time he broke his finger when he had tried to run.

Kids got little scared but Utsav and his team of kids were adamant and convinced others that they could run.

They took the keys of the front door from the unconscious man and opened the door.

The wicked man with big moustache wearing a black coat along with black felt cap opened the door and slapped Utsav hard.

Ujjwal got scared but he was the son of an Army man he hit him hard. As the scene was witnessed by other kids they joined them and hit all of them with the weapons they had in their hands.

Utsav stood up and this time Naina's Taekwondo classes came in handy. She kicked the wicked man hard and Utsav and Manas immediately tied him with the rope he was holding.

They all ran and went out of the ancient place where that lady was waiting along with the policemen.

The policemen congratulated the kids on their defeat to wicked man and thanked them in solving the racket of missing children in Gujarat.

As they all were hugging and smiling they saw their parents along with the police.

All of them were scared but when they saw their parents in tears with a fear in there heart of losing them.

They all rushed towards the open arms of their parents and hugged them tight.

Suddenly, the old woman patted the back of Sankalp as he looked back she gave him the cell of his watch which had fallen at her feet when he had fell while moving towards the cave. Sankalp recalled that incident and smiled while Manas made fun of him stating that he had tried scaring everyone stating it was ghost who had stopped the watch...

They all laughed and for days and day they all were praised for saving so many kids and bringing smile to all the parents who had lost their kids years back.

It was their final exams one more time.

Utsav was in a habit by now of writing his fears and thoughts in a dairy given by his grandfather. He titled this whole incident as an "Unforgettable birthday of my life"

Their intelligence and courage bought all of them back but the most valuable lesson they learnt was that they must listen to their parents and act accordingly as they were not that old after all.

Teenage verses goals

It was the last final exam and Utsav and Ujjwal were excited to be back home only to witness a surprise waiting for them.

Yes, it was their grandparents who had come for a week to meet them along with their paternal aunt and uncle.

Yay! Grandpa, you don't know how much I missed you said Utsav to his grand father

The same words were repeated by Ujjwal too to his grand mother.

They all hugged each other and had lunch.

Sheena said to Virender let us plan a picnic for the family.

Good idea! Said Virender and planned an outing for coming Sunday to Narayan Sarovar and Modhera Sun temple.

What are these places asked Virender's father.

Trust me papa you will enjoy it. Modhera Sun Temple is beautifully designed. It is actually a grand sand stone monument dedicated to Sun God. Utsav intervened, it was built by king Bhimdev of the Solanki dynasty in the year 1026, and elaborate stone carvings are found in every part of the temple. Virender laughed and said let Utsav the encyclopedia guide you then.

Virender's father smiled and said now when you have told me this then also tell me something about Narayan Saarovar too.

Narayan Saarovar is one of the five holy lakes mentioned in Gita. His grandmother intervened and said it is Shrimad Bhagavad-Gita, sorry granny.

Utsav started his sentence again. Narayan Saarovar is one of the five holy lakes mentioned in Shrimad Bhagavad-Gita. It is a sacred pilgrimage site for Hindus.

Very good said his granny while patting his back. Little jealous of everyone praising the elder brother was witnessed by granny in Ujjwal.

What happened to my darling?
Nothing, everyone likes Utsav no one likes me

Who said so.

Everyone is always praising Utsav.

Granny hugged him saying everyone will praise you too if you bring good results in your exam.

You should study hard and you must learn from him instead of getting jealous.

Sorry granny said Ujjwal while hugging her tight.

It was Sunday morning, the car was ready and so was every one to visit Sun temple first thing in the morning.

They reached the Sun temple by 5:30 am, witnessing plenty of people already in line. They all were taking divine bath.

Virender parents felt good and enjoyed morning prayers at temple.

Upon finishing from there they moved towards Narayan Sarovar. The beauty was enchanting. But everyone saw Utsav was not interested in playing with his younger brother, nor he was talking to anyone all he was doing was playing a game on his cell phone.

Grandmother said: My lovely Utsav, go and play with your younger brother he is getting bored.

Utsav ignored his grandmother's order and continued playing on his mobile. That irritated his mother and she immediately snatched the phone from his hand.

Utsav: what are you doing mum?

Sheena: Enough of this damn phone. Go play

Utsav: I don't want to play

Sheena: Then come and sit with us

Utsav made a face and sat with all others

Ujjwal was growing to and his elder brother was his role model. He immediately bought some stones to play but Utsav was angry and he refused to play.

Grandfather asked Utsav: What do you want to do if you don't want to play. When we were of your age we played on national levels and look at you today's generation always playing video games on phones.

I was not playing games on phone I was chatting with my friend.

A friend?

Yes.

Then chat with your friend personally sometimes sending message can be dicey.

No grandfather it's not like that.

When we were of your age we used to meet people in person. Meeting people in person will help you gain more insights my darling and you would learn more.

Utsav did not disrespect his grandfather by replying back but he frowned and sat there quietly. Watching this Ujjwal said to his grandfather, grandpa, it has been long time since we heard story from you.

Utsav immediately said I don't want to hear any story.

To which everyone smiled as they knew it was his teenage and his focus at that time was on his phone.

Virender said if he does not want to hear story let him stay like this. Let me tell you a story today.

You? Papa

Yes why not?

Ujjwal's eyes startled and he lie down on his granny's lap

Virender started, Once upon a time, there was a boy like Utsav who refused to leave his cell phone, wherever he went and his best friend were fed up with this.

Everyone giggled. Utsav looked at his father in dismay.

Shh listen.

He went to a beach along with his best friend and other friends. Everybody left their cell phones at home as they did not want to be disturbed, only that boy took his phone.

They all looked at him but then started playing in water. He was called by his best friend to come and play but he refused stating he was playing his favorite game on phone.

After a while, his friend came and he said he was chatting on phone with another friend through messages just like Utsav was doing.

Utsav groaned, what papa? Why do you have to take my name always?

Virender said nothing personal darling just giving example, you carry on doing what you are doing. He said sarcastically.

Sheena gave him his phone and he started playing on phone.

Everybody was looking at him and Virender said so where were we?

Grandfather said the boy started playing games just like Utsav is doing now.

Ujjwal giggled again

Virender continued. Time passed by and boy grew up. Now his toys had changed, from his phone to his play station to his laptop but he never gave time to his best friend...

But best friends are forever. He kept on calling him to come out and play football but he always said he was busy with his net surfing and chatting or whatever.

After some time, while net surfing he saw his best friend's picture. His best friend by then was a multimillionaire and was an asset to his country. This made him call his best friend.

You never told me, you became such an asset to the country how did you do that?

Simple my friend, I did not waste much of my time on phones and chatting. I was focused moreover I used to meet people in person which gave me insights on where I was focused and see here I am in front of you.

Look at you; do you know where you are?

Yeah, I am also at the top position in a well known company.

To which his friend laughed and said that is my company my friend.

That brought him shame. If he would have concentrated on his studies, met people in person instead of chatting and playing video games he would have been at the same position where his friend was.

Utsav was listening to this story and turned towards his father and apologized. He returned his phone to his mother.

They all had lunch outside and came back.

Soon grandparents left for Delhi and the house was empty one more time. The stories and good food, the chit chat was gone and the usual routine started.

It was time for final results and this time Utsav scored less in his class. But however with bad numbers he passed.

That was a cause of concern for both the parents. They talked to his tuition teacher and school teachers digging the reason behind it.

Everyone said one thing that Utsav keeps on repeating he has knowledge of everything but when it comes to prove he fails.

Virender talked to Utsav of what was bothering him

However, Utsav said the same thing to Virender also. I have knowledge of everything papa don't worry I will come first next time.

That was worrisome for Virender as Utsav refused to talk much on this topic.

The classes started and so were the surprise test that was for the first time that he failed his test.

Virender again asked him, if something is bothering you tell me I am your father.

Utsav was quiet.

He checked his phone and he witnessed his chat with his friend Naveli was more than any other person.

He sat there quietly and explained look young man; you are at the age where you can choose your focus to be distracted by temptations.

Whether it is your first girl friend or smoking or alcohol to prove that you are man enough but to be strong and to be something you need to have focus.

No papa, Naveli is just a friend

I did not take any names young man. I am not scolding you. I am just telling you. We as your parents can show you the path to walk. You as our son can either chose to walk trusting we are there for you or you can fall for temptations thinking they are for you. It is your choice but then do not regret later and come to us asking why we didn't stop you.

Utsav felt his father was talking to him man to man and he is his friend now and said papa, I think I am in love with Naveli.

If it is true love, it can wait and I will be with you to get you married to this girl but not at this stage. Your family is your friend but then we cannot see you spoiling your life.

Finish school and if this girl truly loves you she would wait for you to be something in life. You need to be like your papa young man.

Look at the chart in front of you; you have pasted a picture of a Navy man here why?

Because when I grow up I want to serve Navy papa.

And you think you will join Navy if you fall for the temptations?

Utsav lowered his head and Ujjwal witnessed all this by hiding himself at the corner of the door.

Virender continued, you decided to bring poster of this navy man and I let you because you learnt to put pictures of your goals from whatever site but if you yourself will not follow your goal than we too are helpless.

Come here, Utsav stood up. His father hugged him and left the room.

Ujjwal entered and said Bro, what do I become when I grow up like you?

Utsav smiled and said whatever your heart says.

He kept his father's words in his mind and made a list of temptations which made him out of focus from his goal and decided to be alert.

He wrote about this incident and his father's words in his dairy and read them every day.

Soon he was back being a topper in class again and his father was proud of him. They made him party hard at times but he knew his limits and his goals in life.

Naina and her trip to Manipur

Though Naina was General's granddaughter and was staying with him in Army Cantt, her father was posted in Manipur and her mother was staying with her mother. She was juggling between her husband and Naina.

Naina was a smart girl when she was 7 she often used to hear voices calling her, however upon turning back there would be no one around. When she told her mother about this she ignored it thinking it was Naina's imagination. Now Naina was ten. A grown up girl with responsible attitude. she had almost forgotten about the voices calling her when all of sudden this thing re appeared and she told her mother about it.

Vani was a doctor in Army. She thought that Naina must be missing her papa so she decided to take her along this time to make her meet her father as Diwali was near.

Yuck! Manipur I don't want to go there

What do you know about Manipur?

I know many things why don't you call papa here.

No, we are visiting him. Naina's grandfather hugged her and said young girl experience places, don't assume.

Visit your father. It is just a matter of 10 days. Why are you cribbing so much.

But grand pa Manipur Naina made a rotten face

Her grand pa patted her back and asked her to pack her clothes.

Vani on the other hand was smiling as she would be meeting her husband after a gap of 3 months.

They peacefully left for Manipur.

Naina's father Ashok was waiting for her at the bus stop and as the bus reached he hugged her tightly and welcomed his family to his quarter.

He noticed Naina's sadness. Why are you sad my love asked Ashok

Papa you could have come there. I have so many friends there and they all would be burning crackers without me.

Ashok was a very calm man holding a very good sense of humor.

He said I promise next time I would be there but for this time you can burn crackers with your papa.

She turned her back

Her father knocked her back saying knock knock

She knew this trick as they had played it earlier...

Naina: Who's there?

Ashok: Cows!

Naina: Cows who?

Ashok: Cows go 'moo' not who!

And there was a sudden burst of laugh

For ten days you would enjoy my darling..

Naina felt excited and on the weekend it was planned that they would visit Thalon caves.

Where is Thalon caves papa?

Thalon Caves are locked at an altitude of 900 meters above the sea level at a distance of 4 km from Talon village in Tamenglong district.

Naina's mouth was wide open as she could not understand a word of it.

She questions what are you saying papa

To which Vani intervened, Ashok she is just ten. Don't speak to her like you are speaking to your army officials.

Sorry my mistake dear. Let me explain you in your words.

There is a history behind these caves and I am sure you would love to see it.

Naina sat quietly looking at her papa while holding her favorite doll in her hands

It was discovered by Budhachandra, Maharaja of Manipur in 1946. The caves are one of the main historic sites of Manipur and provide the first concrete evidence of the 2000 year old Hoabhinhain culture in India which is also found in other Southeast Asian Countries.

Now do you understand.

Yes, a little bit

Vani explained further stating there are several caves situated here which are interconnected with each other. To promote tourism, these caves are now part of the Manipur Tourism Festival. The tourism Department arranges for cave expedition in which visitors from all over the world participate.

Ohh so we would be entering those caves alone?

No dear, it is always better to take a guide along to explore the caves.

Why mother?

The darkness and the unknown terrain can be frightening.

How will we go there?

Don't worry darling said Ashok. I have a guide who will take us. It is situated at a distance of 80 km from Imphal, Thalon caves and can be easily reached by trekking which takes around one hour from Thalon village.

Wow!! papa I love discovering and reading about historical places. I think we will have fun.

I know darling it is actually a wonderful place for anthropologists and archaeologists.

I want to be an archeologist when I grow up.

Sure darling, we know where your focus is. Both husband and wife looked at each other and smiled.

The family reached Thalon caves and was enjoying mountain tracking but for Naina it was totally a different experience.

On entering the cave, Naina once again heard a voice calling her name but this time she saw someone behind her and in minutes she saw herself in front of a woman wearing white gown. Her heart was racing fast and she could not open her eyes as the light was too strong for her. Suddenly, she felt a tap on her head and she opened her eyes.

She saw a black woman with shining skin standing in front of her, she was wearing a white dress, and her skin was shining bright. When Naina looked into her eyes she felt peace.

The black woman called herself a fairy god mother.

Naina was inquisitive and curious too.

Aren't godmothers supposed to be white? I mean I have read that in story books.

Fairy God mother laughed and the sound of her laugh was soothing to Naina's ears.

Fairy God Mother said: Now you have seen me hence you too can tell people that God mother is not always white, we don't have colors, we have forms little girl.

Forms?

Yes, we can choose how we should look like

Oh!

You are a special child and we often heard your plea for protection as you could hear voices.

Naina cut her stating but that prayer was for God and not for you.

Fairy God mother smiled and said yes darling. That was for God and we are God's helpers we would help you and teach you how to protect yourself.

Oh! Would I be learning magic?

Fairy God mother smiled and asked would you like to learn magic?

Yes please. But before that can you tell me why you always carry that wand in your hand

Yes my child, Magic wand is a tool of creation, when you use magic with your wand it helps magic happen. Whatever I send out with my magic and with my want it comes back to me.

Oh will I be getting one for myself

No my dear, I would teach you a spell

A spell? What that.
Spell needs a reason; they need a purpose

What is the spell supposed to do. What is it going to create? Without a reason the spell doesn't know what to do

Magic works with the unknown, the unseen. You may not always see the result of your magic spell, magic is mysterious.

It is based on three simple principles

1. Your thoughts create your reality, so you must think positive always
2. Your words create reality, so you must speak kind always
3. Your intentions create reality, so you must intend things carefully.

Think, say and intend with all your heart and your spell will work.

Wow!! That is interesting.

Is it?

Yes

Then I will give you a spell which will give you protection from the voices you hear but use your magic wisely. Help people and yourself with this magic and never hurt another with it otherwise it will come to you in manifolds. Okay?

Naina's curiosity was shining in her twinkling eyes. She immediately promised Fairy God mother that she would follow all the instructions.

I am giving you the strongest spell, I have ever used and I learned it when I was a kid. So it is fitting for you to learn at a young age. Whenever you feel in trouble, whenever you feel you are not safe use this spell.

Repeat aloud if able, if silence is needed repeat the spell in your mind. This is still a spell I say daily before I go to bed.

You?

Yes me. I have used it hundreds of times I was amazed on how safe I am after casting it.

Learn the golden words

I AM A VIOLET BEING OF VIOLET FIRE, THE PURITY THAT GOD DESIRES.

Repeat this number of times until you feel that voices have gone or you feel safe. It helps to imagine yourself being made of violet fire when casting. But it is not required always. This is a very useful spell to practice. Practice it even when you are not in trouble, with practice the spell gets stronger Okay?

Okay fairy god mother.

But how can I meet you again

I will visit you if you would ever be in danger my child. Just remember me in your thoughts.

With these words fairy god mother got vanished and Naina saw herself in her father's lap.

Ashok and Vani were worried on Naina's all of sudden unconsciousness. However they were happy to see that she had gained her consciousness back.

Naina, kept that secret with her and she kept on repeating this spell and with this the voices troubling her vanished off.

She remembered golden rule too and kept on applying that in her life too.

Naina enjoyed her rest of the days with her parents and told her father that she would never forget this place ever.

Parents were happy to see Naina happy.

Responsible with love

As winter approached, Ujjwal being the youngest became lazier than Utsav. He refused to go to school. Many times he used to fake his illness to convince his mother that he was ill but his mother after all understood all his lame excuses.

Okay, if you are not ready to go to school today than I will not share a secret with you

Ujjwal got curious and his drowsy state just vanished and he jumped out of his bed

Mamma please, please tell me what the secret is.

Humm that secret can only open in afternoon if you be a good boy and get ready

Utsav intervened and said Mother I am almost ready you can tell me

No, No if you both want me and your papa to share a wonderful surprise then you have to go to school

Ujjwal jumped from his bed and immediately got ready for the school. The excitement of coming back home for a surprise was more than the lethargy of reaching school.

Ujjwal managed to finish his homework while travelling in school bus. Actually that was the major reason why he didn't wanted to go to school but the excitement of surprise made him finish his homework and he eagerly waited for the clock to wallop one so that he could reach home.

As Utsav and Ujjwal were back their eyes searched for surprise. What can it be?

Mamma, we are back from school. Where is our surprise, please tell us

Quiet both of you. Change your clothes and eat your lunch after that I will tell you

Noooo you said once we are back

Your father is on his way back to home wait for him to come.

Both brothers looked at each other and changed their clothes and ate food as told by their mother.

Mamma, call papa where is he?

I just called him. He has some work in the office and he would be coming back bit late. Since he is the one bringing your surprise you need to complete your homework fast within an hour.

What? Why?

Ummmm because after that you both would not find time to study.

Utsav and Ujjwal finished their homework and revision and waited for their father to come. It was evening by now. Both were looking outside the window disheartened.

Utsav said, come Ujjwal lets go out to play football, papa will come on his usual time only. As Utsav had already given up Ujjwal sat strong saying let's wait for 15 minutes more.

Ujwal saw that Utsav was not listening to him so he proceeded to go out with his football. Being the lovely youngest brother he followed him. As the kids opened the door they saw their father standing and smiling at them while keeping one hand at his back.

The twinkle in the kid's eyes was back. They started jumping and asking for the surprise. As Virender moved his arm forward they saw him holding a little black puppy.

They both hugged their parents and thanked them and immediately started making place for the new member of the family.

Utsav asked his father what we would name him.

Virender smiled and said whatever your heart says kid

Ujjwal immediately came up with the name Twinkle!

Shut up said Utsav it sounds so girlish. He is a boy

After much discussion the puppy was named Leo!

With time, Leo was growing up to be naughty. Some neighbors suggested a Trainer but the love bond between Utsav, Ujjwal and Leo was getting stronger and stronger, the communication between them was not so difficult now.

After 6 months, it was Utsav and Ujjwal's time to take full responsibility of Leo from taking him out for a walk in the morning and evening to his food. Both the brothers started fighting on who would hold the leash and between these fights Leo ran and met a big dog.

Utsav was scared for a while and Ujjwal hid himself behind his brother but the big dog was old he did not say anything to Leo and that brought relief on both the brothers face.

Next it was decided by both the brothers that in morning Ujjwal will take his leash and in evening Utsav and if they were asked to take Leo once they will take turns. Like on Monday Utsav and on Tuesday Ujjwal will handle the leash of Leo.

The whole drama was witnessed by Virender. He smiled and noticed that the boys were becoming more responsible and had also started getting up on time and finishing their homework in time. He also noticed the smile on his wife's face because of Leo and he thanked God for bringing happiness back in his house because of Leo.

Magical Jungle

As the days went by Ujjwal and Utsav were more involved in playing with their furry brother Leo. The morning jogs and the evening runs with Leo not only made their body strong but mind too.

Sankalp was one of those boys who was scared of dogs. He often used to feel annoyed whenever Utsav and Ujjwal would bring Leo along to play football or cricket in the evening.

Why are you so scared of dogs asked Ujjwal from Sankalp?

No, I don't like dogs. When I was young a dog had bit me. This conversation went on and other boys kept on making fun of Sankalp.

Sankalp felt offended and talked to his parents about what happened in the evening.

Sankalp's father asked him to be fearless and not to take anything so seriously …but that did not satisfy the little mind of that boy.

Next day, Ujjwal, Utsav, Sankalp, Manas and Naina met in the school. All friends noticed that Sankalp was maintaining distance from them. During lunch time they all went to him and asked him about his problem and he clearly told them that he was upset about last evening.

Ujjwal hugged Sankalp and apologized for last evening and then all of them hugged him. That brought a smile on Sankalp's face.

As the school bell rang, they all rushed to the bus but unfortunately the bus had some problem They all had to sit inside the school for a while. The authorities were busy informing parents about the problem with the bus. As kids were sitting in the class till the bus got repaired, Ujjwal and his friends squinted towards the jungle from the window of that class, wondering what would be there. The naughtiness in the eyes of all to explore jungle made them break the glass and they all jumped from the window.

They all ran towards the Jungle wondering what it would be from inside.

All the friends were headed by Ujjwal and they kept walking inside the jungle. They heard different voices of different animals which was very scary. Suddenly it was dark inside the jungle and they all decide to go back.

Ujjwal: Let's go back to the school before we get into trouble.

Sankalp and Manas seconded his thought and turned back.

Naina was the one who was supposed to make a mark on every tree while entering into the jungle so that they could go back easily and she was doing that but as they turned back the marks from the trees had vanished. The color of the jungle changed to blue. The trees turned into different color. The jungle was not just a jungle it was a magical jungle.

The kids were not aware of the magic inside the jungle. They were caught up in the web and were scared.

Naina recalled her spell given by the fairy and started reciting that loudly as she wanted to protect her and her friends. No wonder all of them thought that she was being stupid and Ujjwal made fun of her in the midst of fear which irritated Naina and rest was history with the fights making Utsav, Manas and Sankalp being the mediator between them.

Stop fighting idiots said Utsav loudly with fumbled voice. It's time that we find our way back to school.

Let's move towards the left direction as I can hear water running from there said Utsav.

As they moved forward, they witnessed a river that too of green color which astound them.

So, it is only the green water not the road said Manas

Sankalp intervened by telling him that if they follow the water they might end up being near to the road. Utsav is right let us follow the water said Sankalp.

All of them started following the green water

Everyone noticed the water and on mutual agreement started following the flow, they thought it would lead them to road but it led them to a hut. It was already dark, the little bit of sun which they had witnessed while entering the jungle had vanished.

They had no option accept to knock on the door for help.

Naina being the fearless as she had already used to spell of a fairy given to her moved towards the door and knocked. The door was opened by a saint. He looked at all the kids smiling and said come I was waiting for you only, the dinner is ready.

You were waiting for us? Asked Ujjwal in dismay

Yes my child

How did you know we were about to come asked Utsav?

He smiled and said that the blue bird had come and told him. He respectfully asked all of them to have dinner first.

The kids were hungry but were scared too. The saint understood that and said look kids either you spend your night out in the jungle being a food for tiger or you come inside and have dinner and take some rest.

They all looked at each other. Manas being the fattest peeped inside and actually saw food lying on the floor. He jumped inside first which came as a shock to everyone but then they followed him. The kids had good dinner. Ujjwal asked him the way out from this jungle, to which saint said you are tired take some rest we will talk about this tomorrow morning. Sankalp said but our parents must be worried for us by now.

Oh that you should have thought before entering this jungle kid. Go to sleep and we will talk tomorrow. Since all of them were tired they chose to lie down on the floor.

While lying Ujjwal asked does anyone know why the jungle is blue

Utsav questioned Blue? I saw it as yellow

All of them stood up one more time and they all discussed the colors they had seen. The saint was listening to their conversation and asked them to go off to sleep.

They all were quiet missing their family, tears came out from everyone's eyes but since they were tired they all went off to sleep

Around 5 in the morning they all woke up with the sound of OM.

Who is chatting so early asked Naina.

Ujjwal half asleep said of course Saint!! You dumb

I am much more intelligent than you said Naina loudly

Yeah yeah I know said Ujjwal while turning his back towards her.

Utsav woke up by their noise and intervened in-between asking them to stop fighting. Manas and Sankalp were disturbed too and they realized that the chatting of mantra OM was so strong that it was getting inside their heads. Everyone closed their ears and moved out asking saint to stop.

Saint smiled and asked them to join him but they all refused

Ok then bring some wood from the jungle so that I can prepare you some breakfast said saint

Sankalp said sorry sir but we are not here to stay, we want to go home

Exactly said Utsav

Ujjwal requested him to guide the way out from this blue jungle.

He said he will, if only you they would listen and do as he said.

They all agreed.

Manas and Naina cleaned the hut. Sankalp and Utsav go into the right direction and keep walking till you find woods said Saint sternly.

Ujjwal asked and me?

Saint smiled and by holding his hand took him towards the calf and asked him to feed him the grass lying at the backyard.

One by one they all finished what saint had asked them to and went back to him. They saw that the saint was sitting in front of the river with the eyes closed. They all waited for a while but the saint did not move. Ujjwal being the naughtiest touched his eye and whispered in his ear sir we are back are you alive?

Saint smiled with his eyes closed and made them wait. The kids were losing their patience but they saw that the color of the jungle was changing from blue to green to Ujjwal, from yellow to blue for Utsav etc. But they had nothing to do accept wait, they did tried to find their way out by themselves but they couldn't and after returning they found saint sitting in same posture in front of the river.

What is this; where are we and how will we get out of this colorful jungle Manas shouted with fear in his heart and hunger in his stomach. Naina kept on reciting the spell given by the mother fairy. Utsav and Sankalp were praying again to God to help them find the way with tears in their eyes but it was only Ujjwal who went again to saint and asked if he was alive. The saint smiled again but did not move.

Ujjwal got into the hut and saw that the food was ready.

Hey, everyone come here food is ready

Manas ran toward the food followed by others. As they ate the food they immediately felt sleepy and they chose to sleep over there.

This routine continued for two more days... The kids were losing hope but did what saint asked them to do because they all wanted to go home.

On the third day, in the morning, the saint instead of waking kids up with his high vibration chant of OM took everyone's name and they all stood up with a surprise. As they woke up they all started following the routine whereas the saint stopped them.

He asked all of them austerely to sit with him first and chant Om. What Om? We want to go back home sir please our parents must be worried said Sankalp. The saint looked at him smilingly and said until I make you realize the gift inside you; you will not be able to find the way out.

Manas said we don't want gifts we want our way out.

Saint replied you cannot go out unless you recognize that gift within you. That is the reason jungle is holding you. Can't you see.

Ujjwal asked what gift sir? Are you going to give us some gift?

It was for the first time that Saint laughed loudly and asked everyone to close their eyes and chant OM.

They all thought that he was a nerd. They sat and chanted Om. No wonder everyone was looking at saint with one eye open but saint's eyes were closed. After the chant they were asked to run. Manas being the fattest refused, to which saint asked him to finish all the house work on his own without any help?

He looked at Naina but Naina did what saint asked. They all ran and came back, no wonder they did try to find the way out but couldn't.

Manas was tired feeding the calves at the back yard and cleaning the house and bringing the piles of wood but for the saint, he was sitting in front of the river and mediating.

Mansas was very angry and after finishing the work he tried to escape but he could not understand which way to go. The fear of tiger making him his dinner stopped him. As he came back to the hut he saw the food was ready while the saint was sitting in the same position meditating. He could not understand who was making the food? He witnessed a blue bird sitting near the food. That was an unusual dark blue color as he went close by he saw that the bird was looking at him and also she said hi to him and flew away. Manas was amazed.

The kids came back and they all sat down to have food with Manas. Manas told the other kids about how the food was ready as he came back after ten minutes or so. The kids wondered if this saint has another kid as his slave like them and tried to search him but got disheartened.

The night took its turn. Today they were asked to sit outside the hut to witness the moon and stars which for the first time they all saw very clearly. This bought the smile on their faces. And when they went inside like always the food was ready.

The saint told them that he does not have any other kid as a slave and they are free to go the way they are trying to run for past three days.

The kids were shocked wondering how he knew what they were talking and doing,

But you were out there with your eyes closed said Naina

The way you chant om with your one eye open, I know everything what you say and do with my both eyes closed. I am only trying to help. If you don't want you are free to go.

They all were ashamed of their behavior and apologized saying they will do what he will ask them to do.

From the next day, they did not cheat the saint and did what he asked them to.

Few days passed and they all got so engrossed with the daily activity that the thought of leaving this place was out from their minds. Unknowingly, every day by meditating OM first thing in the morning they were learning to focus. The saint further helped them on sixth day by telling them that how their focus was increasing. He even made them realize that the jungle was not colorful anymore.

Wow, everything is so normal said everyone with a twinkle in their eye.

On the sixth day, the saint taught them to direct their energies on what they wanted.

Ujjwal asked how?

To which he replied. Listen carefully kids, sometimes you hate a particular subject in school let's say Naina hates Hindi or Ujjwal hates science or Utsav hates his French classes or Sankalp hates math, I am just giving you an example.

By hating that subject you are putting your negative energies in that subject which makes it more difficult and you end up bringing less numbers in that subject while excelling in the subject you love the most because you put so much of positive energy in that subject it shows you everything to be very simple and direct, you find it easy to remember.

Naina asked what energy?

Focus of not liking something whether subject or human. When you don't like it you go and tell everyone that this subject is bad or the teacher of this particular subject is bad towards you but in reality, you are the one giving negative energy to them and your focus on something which is not good will only make you see things which you don't like.

Utsav intervened asking I cannot understand.

Utsav my child it is very simple, you hate this jungle right?

Sankalp said yes

Why do you hate it?

Because we are not able to get back

What kind of energy you are giving out to this jungle

Naina said that we don't like you

Exactly then what this jungle is giving you back

Ujjwal said nothing

No, this jungle is blocking your way back home saying I don't like you too. You all see it in different colors everyday not normal which is suffocating, Right?

The kids kept on thinking about it the whole day sitting outside and discussing.

They went back to Saint and asked what we should do now

Simple stop giving negative energy

How

Stop cribbing. Stop discussing saying how bad is this jungle that it made you lose your way back home.

Ujjwal then how this jungle will show us the way back home?

Saint smiled and said your focus of what is wrong will show you only wrong and your focus on good will show you good. Like every day you wake up and recite OM at that time you forgot about the jungle and it showed you pure sunlight on the 5th day isn't it? Go to sleep now. The kids slept while thinking of what saint had taught them.

For another two days none of them spoke or cribbed about the jungle. They continued with the routine.

As the chanting of mantra Om was regular for more than a week now, the kids were becoming more peaceful and were able to rely on their gut feeling. They were no more restless.

Like every day they chanted the Mantra OM. Ujjwal had a thought of Leo while chanting mantra and was smiling with his eyes closed.

Suddenly, everyone heard a bark; it was Leo outside the hut who called for him. They all looked at saint and smiled, the saint asked them to go out. They all stood up and ran outside.

Yes, it was Leo, Ujjwal and Utsav cried and hugged and kissed their furry brother. Leo directed all of them way back which was just two minute walk from the hut. They all were surprised and looked at each other wondering why they could not find the way earlier. To which Naina repeated saint's golden words "your focus of what is wrong will show you only wrong and your focus on good will show you only good."

Yes, we all had stopped cursing jungle and then jungle showed us way out.

Manas said shall we go back and thank the saint. We moved out in a hurry without bidding him goodbye. After all he gave us food and shelter for so many days. As they all decided to turn back they saw saint waving them goodbye. They all saw their parents with police standing outside the jungle. While some policemen were directed inside the jungle to find them. Parents saw their kids coming along with Leo and they all hugged their kids. The kids were happy to be back.

They never returned to the jungle ever again but the lesson which saint gave them helped them all in bringing good marks in the subject they hated the most. But for Sankalp, he realized that it was not wise to hate Leo. After all it was Leo who brought him back to his parents and he hated him the most. He started feeding stray dogs keeping his fear aside realizing what we focus on excels.

Every evening kids and Leo used to play football and Leo was hero for all of them.

Merry Christmas

Come December, come holidays. The Christmas celebrations had begun and the chief minister of the state was invited to speak to the kids on Christmas. Since the school was of the Christian origin with the motto to "Love & Serve one another" Joy was all around. Kids were happy because for the first half of the day there were no classes. Soon Security guards were alerted. From 1st to 12th all classes were asked to be seated in a hall. The programme was to start with the speech given by the Minister.

Respected Principal, Faculty members and young stars of this school:

First of all, I would like to thank you for giving me an opportunity to stand in front of you today.

Today, we gather here to celebrate the spirit of Christmas. Christmas celebrates the birth of Jesus. The Gospel of John says that Jesus came from God to bring his "Word" or message to all people and that message is clearly drawn on the motto of the school that is "Love Serve one Another".

My dear kids, It is believed by every child that Santa comes to them on 24ᵗʰ December night and leave gifts for them. I am here to tell you that Santa does come and it is not just a fable. He stays with you every time, in the form of your teachers and parents to educate you towards your bright future. One day when you finish your education and move from this school, you might become Prime minister, President, Engineer or Doctor. Trust me at that time you will look back and thank each one of those who stood by you and offered you the gift of teaching, whether it was one boring subject or happy learning times. They educated you. They helped you to become who you are and then you would realize that Santa actually never left you. You never had to wait for 24ᵗʰ December night for him to come, he was, in fact he is with you guiding you towards your bright future as a gift always.

When I squinted at the invitation which was extended to me I was glad to notice that this school supports girl child education and soon going to open another branch that would only be for girls. In today's era, supporting girl child education is a must. Education is very important for all. It is sad that some communities still discriminate against the education of the girl child. An African proverb says, "If we educate a boy, we educate one person. If we educate a girl, we educate a family – and a whole nation." By sending a girl to school, she is far more likely to ensure that her children also receive an education. As many claim, investing in a girl's education is investing for a nation.

I personally feel that supporting girl child education brings lots of benefits like:

- Educated women are more likely to participate in political discussions, meetings, and decision-making, which in turn promotes a more effective world
- Educated girls and women are less likely to be victims of domestic harassment and sexual violence in their societies.
- Educated women have a greater chance of escaping poverty, leading healthier and more productive lives, and raising the standard of living for their children, families, and communities.
For every one boy that is educated, each and every girl should be educated too.

I personally wish the best of luck to the school in supporting girl's education and wish them success in future endeavor. And to you, my dear young friends, I wish you bright future and may Santa be with you all the time to guide you towards your goal and gives you the gift of light peace and security which helps you in spreading love and light in this world

Thank you and merry Christmas to all of you.

As he finished his speech the students started clapping. The secretary of the minister whispered something in his ear which made minister restless and he immediately left the stage and asked the principal to speak to him in private.

Later he came back to stage and said: - My dear kids, we have just received an information that terrorists have entered our territory, I would request all of you to leave together after the school and reach home safely. Thank you. The minister immediately left for his office to investigate further on this information.

Kids were not bothered about it. All they wanted was to enjoy and soon after the programme lunch hour bell rang. The school kids were excited and Rohan and his friends were making plans during lunch hour on how they will be celebrating Christmas this year.

Just 1 more day of school and then we will be free yay said Rohan

Manas: Hey we will do pizza party at my house

Ujjwal had some other plans so he asked why not party outside we will have momo's and burger

Not a bad idea said Naina

Utsav intervened by saying that parents will get angry if we made a plan to go out...

Naina: we will take permission or let it be at house only. Eh yew my mom gave me round gourd for lunch

Rohan said yeah, you know I have lady finger in my lunchbox to eat yuck!

Manas said my mother gave me spinach.

Ujjwal laughs and said I don't know when our parents will understand that we don't like to eat these vegetables; by the way I saw one white hair in your head Naina.

Ujjwal's joke irritated Naina and the fight started where Manas asked them to be quiet.

Utsav said but I enjoy eating lady finger sometimes... the naughty smile on his face was clearly showing his cute lie and everyone together said yeah yeah we know... Discussion continued till the bell rang.

It was last period and the fish market in class room was on when suddenly principal, class teacher and a stranger entered the classroom.

Class teacher grabbed the attention of everyone by clapping and shouting Class silent...

The classroom was silent like a meditation room.

Principal said Kids, in these winter holidays we have a task for you, and everyone was given a form from the stranger who was a member of an NGO. The form clearly asked for the donation for the under privileged kids.

The stranger gave brief introduction to the kids about the organization. He told them that the foundation is a non-profit organization in India. The organization strives to fight issues like hunger and malnutrition in India. By implementing the

Mid-Day Meal Scheme in the Government schools and Government aided schools, we aim to fight not only hunger but also to bring children to school.

Everyone took the form and kept it in the bag as an assignment to do. As the bell rang all of them took their bags and ran towards the school bus.

Ujjwal asked Rohan Buddy, What is that mid day meal scheme he was talking about

Rohan shrugged his shoulders and said leave it for holidays. Tell me are you coming to play football in the evening.

Utsav said yes. We all will meet at the club.

As the discussion for meeting in the evening was going on between the kids, the bus was stopped by three terrorists and they forced the driver to take the bus to a lonely place. From midway terrorists sent driver back to the school asking him to tell the school authorities that the kids were with them and they will soon contact the school for ransom.

The kids started crying. Their heartbeat was racing fast. The terrorists asked the kids to get out of the bus one by one while holding a gun in his hands.

The kids were scared and refused to get out of the bus when suddenly one of the terrorist shot the teacher in her leg and threw her out of the bus, as she was not listening to them and was trying to grab attention of public by shouting. The bus was forcefully taken to their hub which was somewhere inside the jungle but not far away from the road.

Every kid was scared. The kids did as the terrorists asked them to. Crying, hungry and scared they did not know whom they should look upon.

The kids were kept in a hut locked from outside.

It was almost dawn. There was no arrangement of food for the kids. They all saw from the window that terrorists were partying. They all were hungry and they looked into their bags for food. All they had was leftover food in the lunch box which they had refused to eat during lunch hour as they detested the taste of it. This made them realize the value of food which their parents gave them every day.

Night went by and the kids were not aware of what was happening outside.

The Terrorist asked for 25 Lakh from the parents to release the kids and the parents were worried on other side.

The kids were not offered food the next morning too. The motive behind not giving them food was to weaken their energy so that they would not run. Some of the kids were losing hope.

In the afternoon, the terrorist gave them only bread piece to eat. No wonder Ujjwal, Utsav and Naina being the kids of the army man decided to accomplish this mission and to help other kids to go back home.

During the evening, when kids saw that the other terrorists were out to fetch food for themselves leaving one of them to guard, they made a plan

Ujjwal requested one of the terrorist who was sitting outside the hut to open the door as he wanted to pee.

No wonder the terrorist disregarded his plea and the plan failed. After a while, Naina started shouting from inside. The terrorist tried to peep from the window but he could not see anything. He shouted from outside asking what had happened to which Manas replied that the girl had some panic attack and the other kids started making sound as if they were crying.

The terrorist had to open the door. As he opened the door Ujjwal and Utsav hit him hard with their bags and the other kids ran from that place towards the road.

As the terrorist was beaten brutally by the kids he could not even stand. Naina immediately closed the door of the hut and locked him inside.

The police was patrolling on the road and saw the students running on the road. They helped them and made arrangements to send them back to their home and with the information given by the kids the terrorists were caught.

The very same night when everyone reached home safely, Rohan's mother bought lady finger for him to eat. As the plate was in front of him he looked at the food and tears started rolling from his eyes.

I don't have Friends here

Naina was the only girl in Ujjwal's group of friends. She often used to feel ignored and affronted by Ujjwal's behavior. As hardly other friends used to take her side in front of Ujjwal. But she was a fighter and she used to fight her battles hard but her heart was somewhat lonely seeking friends.

Since the holidays were on, the kids either used to play or sleep. One afternoon, Naina's mother noticed that she came early holding a tiny stray puppy in her hands. She wanted a friend and here it was. She told her mother that the group of boys was making fun of her and cried inconsolably, cribbing about the rude behavior of other kids to her.

My lovely doll, first tell me where did you find this puppy.

Oh! She was outside our house I have named her Miranda.

You have your stray pet Miranda outside the house; play with her when you don't feel like going out with your other friends.

Miranda is not my friend. She is just an animal and that too stray.

No Naina, never say like this. The most faithful friend of human is dog. The way you feel betrayed by your friends, they too, sometimes. The way you feel loved and wanted by your papa and mummy they too feel the same. The only difference is the way they communicate.

Naina's mother could notice that Naina was not happy with what she had just told her
The mother then took her head into her lap and said: Okay, let me tell you a story.
Once there was a spoilt princess who had all her wishes fulfilled easily and her friends were not her true friends. They just used to heed every command of her because she was a princess.

One day she realized this and became sad and depressed. She went to her parents and said, I have so many friends but nobody talks to me. Everyone let's me win and I never know how it is to have real friends, I feel so sad.

Her parents did not know how to find the solution of her problem so they asked a healer to come to heal her depressive mood. The healer said your majesty; there is one remedy that could help the princess.

King: "Please tell us sir, we will do anything for our daughter"

The healer asked the King to send her to the farms and to make sure that she spends her time with nature and animals around.

Heeding up to the advice the princess was sent to the farms with her attendants where she had her new friends, the animals! Chickens! Horses! Cows! Goats! Fishes!

The princess was happy and told her parents, this is so much fun I love all these farm animals! But the horse is my favorite! I love washing him, brushing his mane and petting him!

After many days of spending time with farm animals her parents noticed she was a cheerful child again.

Princess said to her father that the animals were her best friends! She told him that they are so innocent and full of joy! That she loved them.

On listening to this story Naina asked her mother can we keep Miranda in our house like Ujjwal has Leo
Naina's mother smiled and said my darling, the stray animals are not vaccinated and these innocent beings while playing can sometimes bite which can cause rabies hence we need to get her to the doctor first.

Naina nodded her head in agreement. Naina's mother asked her to invite Ujjwal and her other friends at home for a little party.

The girl asked the boys to come to her place at five in the evening. Everyone nodded in agreement and visited her place exactly at five.

The chocolate yogurt pops were waiting for all of them.

The kids were happy and Naina had fun in the evening while partying around with them.

As Manas was curious about the recipe so that he could also make it at home. Naina told him the recipe.

All you need is:-

8 ounces plain nonfat yogurt.
¼ cup sugar-free cocoa mix
4/6 ounce paper cups.

Combine yogurt and cocoa in a bowl and mix well. Spin into paper cups and set the cups in a muffin tin. Insert a wooden Popsicle stick in the middle of each cup. Freeze until it becomes solid. Simple peel away the paper cup while serving.

Interesting Naina, I will make this for my parents as a surprise tomorrow morning. Will you help me asked Manas To which Utsav and Ujjwal laughed but Naina ignored their laugh and agreed to help Manas.

The day went happily and Naina realized that pets are our true friend and we must not seek friendship everywhere. A true friend always stays.

Ujjwal the super man

S ince the winter vacations were on, Sheena wanted to visit her parents staying in Mumbai. Virender could not get leave from his job hence they decided that Sheena along with Ujjwal and Utsav would visit her parents while Leo would stay back with Virender.

Two days trip from Gujarat to Mumbai was planned. Utsav and Ujjwal were very happy and excited to meet their cousin Vikram at maternal grandparent house.

They reached Mumbai without knowing what could be waiting for them, They were happy to meet their cousin Vikram who was the boy for Sheena's brother. Vikram showed them his winning trophies for his football tournament. They discussed how their life was different from his in Gujarat.

Vikram said I want to play football for my country. What are your ambition he asked from Utsav and Ujjwal. Then Utsav said I want to work for Indian Navy. Little Ujjwal was blank and said he had not decided as yet.

While spending the day, they saw that their mother was sleeping since morning so the boys spent some time with grandparents. Utsav asked his grandmother, Granny why mumma is sleeping since morning is she alright. To which granny laughed and replied because now she is with her momma and her mumma is taking care of her like she takes care of both of you. She is resting as she is tired.

Ujjwal immediately asked why tired. We are not tired.

Because she does all house work in Gujarat on her own. You two boys do not help her.

The boys looked at each other and asked what can we do for her.

Help her in making food. Learn to make simple food. Sometimes she too needs a break. How many times you clean your room, or help her in making food during holiday, asked granny to which both the boys looked each other and Vikram instantly said I do it every time. Sometimes I surprise my mother by making tea for her.

Now he is being proud. He is trying to be an all rounder. He plays football. He is good in studies and now he knows cooking also thought Ujjwal.

The jealousy between the siblings was imminent

Disregarding the ongoing conversation the boys kept quiet and said lets go out and play.

Vikram introduced them to his friends. While playing suddenly they heard a voice of someone shouting. All of them including people of society followed the voice. It was of a woman whose girl had suddenly gone missing.

My girl Arushi. She was just playing outside, I don't know where she went, please help me find her.

Everyone looked around, the police also came. But it was almost evening, they could not locate the girl.
Ujjwal was the only boy in his friends who was heeding up to the advice of the saint he met up in magical jungle. Every morning after waking up he used to chant OM, the vibrations of Om had made him very intuitive. He was not aware that his gift of telepathy had been activated.

Suddenly, he heard a girl's cry asking for help and his gut feeling told him that the girl would be in the nearby park. He asked his brother and his cousin Vikram to come along. As they went inside the park, Vikram started shuddering with fear. What happened? Why are you shivering asked Utsav

Nothing, I think we should go back.
Why what is wrong with this park asked Ujjwal

No one comes here, this park is haunted. Who so ever entered this park gets lost. We must go back. It is locked by the society people. We should avoid going into it more

Then I am sure this girl Arushi must be here only said Ujjwal and he climbed inside along with his brother. Watching their brave act, Vikram too climbed inside.

The park was not at all maintained. Ujjwal touched the dead shrubs. As he was touching the shrub a male voice asked him "who are you" "Don't Touch and get out of here".

Vikram hid himself behind Utsav but fearless Ujjwal asked him why should we leave. Who are you? Come in front of us.

The mail voice laughed hysterically and asked them one more time to leave or they will be killed.

The kids got scared but Utsav intervened saying we are not going anywhere until you tell us who you are?

I am the king of this park, I stay here.

Okay, we just want to know is Arushi with you asked Ujjwal

He laughed again with a warning.

The boys were adamant and they forced him to reply. He confirmed that the girl was with him but in his heart of hearts decided to kill these boys too and said let me play a game with you people.

For every correct answer you will be led to my palace inside this ground and for every wrong answer these shrubs will hurt you.

Without thinking twice, Ujjwal agreed to it. It was almost dark and Vikram stopped him to which he said: Come on we have you. You are genius and perfect in everything, you will help us. Utsav nodded in agreement.

They moved forward and said okay we are ready.

The Evil man's voice asked them. Tell me what is the name of a prickly pear cactus.

Ujjwal and Utsav look at Vikram for an answer but poor Vikram was scared and sweating.

Utsav immediately replied it is called Opuntia.

Good the voice replied. Scared Vikram asked Utsav what is Opuntia to which Ujjwal replied that it is a part of the cactus family. Prickly pears are native only to the Americans, but they have been introduced to other parts of the globe too.

The voice said hummm so we have intelligent boys here and suddenly they went under the grass where they found themselves in a dark hollow tunnel. They walked into that tunnel holding each other hand and suddenly the voice said STOP

You need to answer some more questions what is the hurry?

Tell me what is as big as an Elephant but weighs nothing. Vikram enthusiastically said I know it is our body weight to which the tunnel started shaking and Vikram started bleeding from his left arm.

The voice got angry and said wrong answer I am giving you last chance. To which Utsav instantly replied it is Shadow

The voice calmed down and they were showed a door. Ujjwal knocked the door and they heard the cry of the girl.

The voice asked. Your next answer will either lead you to the girl or to your death. So be careful in replying.

The boys became nervous and nodded in agreement.

The voice asked them which animal can live longest without water?

Ujjwal knew it and he replied instantly with a smile Rats.

Good going, the door opened and they saw a girl in a cage ready to be food of an evil.

The girl was in tears while the boys were happy that they had found her. Utsav reached towards the girl and tried to open the cage.

The voice they had been hearing appeared in front of them wearing a black robe and said not so easily boys.

Tell me now. A paddling is a group of which animals?

They all were quiet and looked at each other in fear of what will happen next. To this the girl replied Ducks

The Evil got angry and asked her to shut up while saying if you want this girl to be out. This is your last chance.
A muster is a group of which birds?
Utsav looked at him saying peacocks.

The Evil said: I am impressed. I like intelligent kids hence you all will stay here along with her and he laughed.

With the Chanting of mantra OM everyday Ujjwal's vibration of the body had become strong and protective

Ujjwal interrupted his laugh and stepped in front of him saying that means you are not the one who would keep your word.

As evil saw Ujjwal radiating white light strongly he got agitated with the courage of the boys and all of sudden the whole palace of evil started shuddering. The evil said nobody argues with me, no kid till date dares to speak with me like this. No one can stand in front of me so bravely like this who are you? Why I am losing my powers?

As the whole area was shuddering and falling all over they suddenly saw themselves out in the park along with the girl.

Vikram taped on the shoulder of Utsav and pointed towards the sky. The white beam covered the whole park. Suddenly, the dead shrubs and trees came to life and they saw the evil in the black robe along going towards the light.

A gently voice of a lady said this evil was no one but fear. No one till date could conquer him and I am proud of you all. Now this area is clear from the negative energy hence kids can come and play here whenever they want.

The white light was witnessed by society people also and they all ran towards the park. Aarushi's mother saw her and hugged her tight. They all thanked the boys. Utsav ended up being Aarushi's new friend whereas Ujjwal pated on his cousin's shoulder and said that I have decided what I will be when I grow up.

Utsav and Vikram looked at him and he said I will be a good, helpful man to all. Utsav intervened saying my brother you are my Superman. I am so very proud of you.

They all reached home and told their families of what exactly had happened. Vikram who was so proud of his trophies and achievement said I am proud to be Utsav and Ujjwal's brother and never ever I will show off my achievements which could make others feel less in front of me.

They all became hero of the society that night and celebrated their victory over evil.

On reaching back Gujarat, Utsav and Ujjwal decided to help their mother sometimes with the housework and the first thing they learnt was to make tea for their parents.

The ring of the Golden Bell

School decides to take students on educational tour. They decided to visit Kodaikanal a hill station in the taluk division of the Dingigul district in the state of Tamil Nadu in India. Its name in Tamil means "The Gift of the Forest".

The kids were very happy as they were on their first train journey towards Tamil Nadu. All the kids were near about twelve years of age.

Naina: I am so excited to visit this place

Ujjwal: Good. Me too

Naina:, Do you know that Kodiakanal is referred as the "Princess of Hill station" and has long history. Manas intervened and said enough of the history Naina, get ready. We have to take bus from the coming station the teachers are asking everyone to take their bags.

Naina smiled and ran towards her seat. She wore her shoes and stood with Manas and Ujjwal near the train gate along with other students.

They took a bus to reach Kodaikanal. As the kids were watching out from the window of the bus Manas was very excited and he was jumping in the whole bus disturbing students around.

As they reached the destination, to their surprise there school friend in other bus had reached the place before them. Everyone knew that. Naina and Ujjwal were not good friends and used to fight all the time and at that time same thing happened.

Teachers had to intervene and ask them to apologies to each other. The whole bunch of kids were directed to "Hotel Villa Retreat" surrounded by beautiful red flowers and exotic views.

Next day, all the students and teachers enjoyed visiting Shembaganur Museum of natural history and as Naina was a sucker of history she enjoyed watching their outstanding taxidermy collection of more than 500 species of animals, birds and insects and a living collection of over 300 exotic orchid species.

They were having fun, while watching the other tourist attractions. All of sudden Naina realized that Ujjwal was missing. She immediately diverted everyone's attention towards Ujjwal and everybody started searching for him. While his brother Utsav was crying hard the disoriented teachers showed pictures of Ujjwal to people around but no one had seen the kid.

It was getting dark. One of the teacher brought all the other kids back to the house while other teachers were in police station reporting for the missing case.

Manas, Utsav and Naina were in deep shock and decided to stay together that night while discussing what could have happened to Ujjwal.

Next morning, Manas woke up before dawn and saw from the window of the hotel that a man wearing a big robe of black color who was hiding his face inside the robe was looking towards the window of his room.

Manas immediately woke Naina and Utsav and all the three kids looked at that man. Naina being the brave among all immediately shouted from the window itself. As the teacher approached the kids, the man in the robe vanished in split second.

Manas, Utsav and Naina looked at each other befuddled and got ready to reach police station along with the teachers. Unfortunately, there was no news of Ujjwal....

Ujjwal's brother could not sleep the whole night and when he heard the inspector he could not control his tears and started crying. When kids saw him in tears they also started crying out of fear.

Vijay, the school teacher saw this and decided to take the kids to Bryant Park situated close to the Kodai Lake so that he could divert their minds from this issue.

The kids hired bicycles and Vijay and the other teacher chose to walk. Utsav noticed the man with the black robe again standing at the corner of the lake.

Utsav immediately stopped Manas and Naina and asked them to look at the corner. The moment three of them looked at him the man with the robe vanished.

Utsav: I just saw him trust me, he was here

Manas: maybe he is trying to scare us

Naina: May be he wants to talk to us or he has some clue where Ujjwal is

As the three of them were discussing amongst each other they heard a cry of a woman. Another kid had got lost while riding a horse.

What is happening over here said Vijay and immediately took all the kids back to the hotel.

They reached hotel and from the window they kept on waiting for the man with the black robe but he did not appear that day.

Disheartened kids went back to sleep. As they were sleeping they all had a dream that Ujjwal was standing near water fall crying for help and they were trying to help him but he got lost again. In all this they saw the board of Bear Shola Falls.

When they woke up they discussed with each other the dream that they all had seen last night.

Utsav: how can all of us have the same dream? Manas and Naina looked at each other confused.

Naina approached the teacher and asks her if there was any place called Bear shola falls. Teacher enquired with the hotel waiter and he confirmed the name of the place. The kids then asked their teachers to take them there. However they were scared to take them out of the hotel but after thinking hard they did take them to enjoy the waterfall in the reserve forest.

All of sudden, three of them heard someone applauding and they turned their head only to witness a woman with wicked looks wearing the black robe in front of them. This time the teacher and other kids were untraceable.

The heart of the kids started racing fast. Utsav being the eldest tried to talk to her.

Who? Who are you?

Where are our teachers? How are we here in this cave?

Shhhhhhh said the woman. I do not like too many questions in one time. You are here because I called all of you and you came on your own.

Manas started crying but Naina and Utsav were among the bravest of all. We never came here on your call witch shouted Naina and started reciting her spell which Fairy God mother had given it to her earlier

No use of shouting and showing your anger, nobody will listen here accept me and your spell will not work here. I am the most powerful witch. This is my Kingdom and yes you are here because I called you. Remember, all of you had that same dream of your friend near water fall.

She clapped again and the wall turned into a T.V in which they saw their friend.

All of them started shouting his name and the witch laughed.

They noticed that along with Ujwal there were other kids too.

She clapped one more time and they saw all the kids being torched by other witches.

What do you want from us asked Utsav.

She looked and him and tried to scare him but he was brave. She looked at Manas and he again started crying hiding behind Naina.

She laughed and laughed and all of sudden she said, I will tell you what I want if you answer my questions.

The looked at each other and Naina asked her what questions?

Simple questions. I want to test your general knowledge

Go ahead said Naina

Hummm, Okay She clapped again and she got a lily flower in her hand.

Look at this carefully and tell me what is it?

Manas started giggling and said very funny. Everyone knows that this is Lilly

Oh you little boy you know how to giggle too

Yes you are right this is Lilly

Tell me, the name of the plant which can hold a human hand, as well as the rest of the 300 Lb human body?

Three of them started looking at each other.

Utsav said I know. I have read it somewhere but the name oh God help me

No, here no God can come to you. You have to help yourself

Naina looked into the witch's red eyes and said it is called Victoria Amazonica

Yes, that is the name said Utsav and let me tell you the plant is not only large, but it changes colours. When its flowers blooms on the first night, they are of pure white color but the next day they turn into pink colour.

Hum, intelligent kids... My next question is for your cry baby friend Manas. Tell me young boy how many years are there in a millennium?

Ha, 1,000 that is easy.

The witch looked into his eyes to make him fearful and asked him another question

Scarlet is of bright red color... True or false

Manas being fearful answered bravely True.

The witch laughed again and became silent all of sudden pointing fingers on these three kids.

I will tell you what I want, if you get me what I want I will leave your friend and all the other kids I have here with me.

She asked them to bring a Golden Bell from the Forests.

But how would we look for it asked Naina

That is not my concern. My people will take you to the forest. After that it is your journey towards the Golden Bell and if you tell anyone that I have asked you to bring that I will kill all the kids.

Three of them looked at each other and nodded in yes to her.

She asked them to close their eyes and the next moment when they opened their eyes they were in the forest. The darkness scared the kids but they were there for their friend Ujjwal. They had to bring him back at any cost.

As they took a step further they heard a roar of a lion. All three of them hugged each other and hid themselves behind the tree.

Then suddenly they heard a voice asking them how they were here. They looked around and no one was there. But soon that tree turned into a dwarf, I am the one who is asking you, they got scared and screamed.

The dwarf asked them to calm down and promised them to help.

Manas told him that they were here to find the golden bell.

The astounded dwarf asked them to follow him.

Soon they saw themselves entering into the village of dwarves and the head of Dwarf asked them why they were searching for the bell?

Three of them stood straight with their heads down.

Humm, I can only help you if you tell me the truth.

Manas then squinted at the Dwarf and said if we tell you the truth she will kill our friend Ujjwal.

Dwarf understood that by She they meant the witch who had been trying hard to get the Golden Bell but he kept quiet as he knew that the little kids were being followed by the witch.

He said it is not easy to get the Golden bell, to get it you have to maneuver your ways through the maze.

Naina questioned what maze are you talking about?

The old Dwarf smiled and said as you move forward you would be guided.

He asked the dwarf to take them towards the open sky as their journey would begin from there.

The dwarf then asked them to close their eyes again and the next moment when they opened their eyes they were out of the forest in a place where nothing was around, all they could see was that the clouds were coming down…

A sweet voice welcomed them. So you are here to search for the Golden Bell

Manas answered in affirmation.

As he said yes, one of the cloud coming down turned into a beautiful white woman with golden hair. She was wearing White blouse and White skirt...

I can guide you further if only you answer my question.

What question asked Utsav

What comes down but never goes up?

Three of them started thinking hard.

The girl in white giggled and says you do not have much time, I have to go, I can give you my introduction as a hint. I am the princess in clouds land

Manas immediately answers it's the Rain...

Yes, you are brilliant Manas

Thanks but how do you know my name

She smiled and gave him a ring while asking all of them to close their eyes

Next moment when they opened their eyes they were in front of a river.

Three of them looked at each other and cribbed. What is this nonsense every time they asks us to close our eyes the next moment we are somewhere else said Utsav. I am worried how my brother would be...

Naina intervened and said angrily moreover they keep on asking so many questions

Forget everything and look at this golden ring which she has given me.

The witch was watching all of them till they received the Golden Ring, once it was in the hands of the kids her power failed to observe them further.

She could not enter the pious forest herself as the negative was banished instantly. She got furious, never a kid could cross Drawfs these three kids were special, how come they had reached the next level.

Here as the kids were cribbing in front of the sea, the white man with the beard came out of the sea and got upset with them...

How did you come here young kids? You have disturbed my sleep.

Ah, uncle we are here in search of a Golden Bell said Utsav

The old man laughs and says that stupid witch must have sent you. Right?

Yes uncle

Get lost! Go back there is no golden bell here...

Utsav starts crying and says please don't say like this uncle. If we are unable to find that bell she will kill my brother. Manas and Naina intervened saying and his brother is our best friends. His name is Ujjwal.

Why should I help you said the old man

Naina comes in front and says because you look like my grandfather and my grandfather always loved kids

Those sweet words softened his heart and he looked at the ring which was already given to Manas by the princess of cloud's land.

My dear kids, if she gets the Golden Bell she would destroy all goodness, nonetheless I cannot see you crying.

He takes the water from his hand and soon that water turns into star fish.

Naina, Utsav and Manas's eyes widened and started twinkling

He smiled and says while giving one to each, keep this with yourself always as it will remind you about the goodness stored in your innocent heart, The way you have reached here you would reach the golden bell too...

They all took the starfish and immediately closed the eyes

The old man asks why you are closing your eyes I did not ask you too

Utsav being the naughtiest by nature says well, everyone asks us to close our eyes after giving gifts.

HAHAHA they asks you to close your eyes because magic cannot be seen my dear, it can be felt.

Go straight from here and turn towards left and remember there is no place for fear here.

The thanked him and started walking. Manas being the cutest fat boy said what bro now we have to walk.

Naina says it is good for you.

Utsav while looking at the star fish cracks a joke.

Do you know Naina what does one star say to another when they meet?

No, I don't know

Manas, do you know

No, I don't know too

Glad to meteor!

All of them laughed only to meet another challenge on the way

They saw a house made up of gold where the golden bell was hanging without a ring

Wow what a house says Utsav

Manas felt scared to move ahead

Naina noticed and reminded the old man's golden words "There is no place for fear"

The moved toward the house. As they were about to touch the fence they were stopped by the dog.

Hey, who are you? What are you doing here?

A dog can talk?

The kids were experiencing mesmerizing things

Yes, in my world I can talk.

We are here to take the Golden bell says Naina

Humm, what are your names?

They all introduce themselves and the Dog introduced himself as Oreo.

The big black Labrador took them inside his house and offered them juice

Naina felt Oreo's moves clever and told him that they did not need juice they were okay, but Manas does not heed up to Naina's call and immediately finished all of the grape juice and sleeps there.

Utsav tried hard to wake Manas up but he was in deep sleep.

The dog laughs and says what made you think that you can get the golden bell so easily to your world.

As Naina had been learning karate in her school she calls the dog for fight.

The dog roars but Naina was not scared meanwhile Utsav tries to wake Manas up.

Are you not scared of me I can kill you with my paw

No, I am ready for a fight says Naina

The dog asks her to calm down and applaud her fearless attitude. At the same time he warns her about the witch.

With his one bark Manas wakes up and they were lead to the Golden Bell

Hey, but wait you do not have the ring without that it would not make a sound says Oreo

Manas immediately showed him the ring and attached it to the bell.

Now when you ring it, it would lead you to the place you came from but be careful about the motives of the witch.

They all thank Oreo and rang the golden bell.

The witch heard the ring of the golden bell and rejoiced in happiness. All the kids were in front of her.

Good give this to me Naina.

No, we want you to free all the kids first.

The witch was not of her words she tries to harm them with her magical nails but the kids were supported by the goodness in their hearts and the magic which they had brought for themselves from the other world.

What all of you have bought from that world that my magic is not working? Come on, show me what is it?

Three of them together took the star fish out from their pockets and the luminous light came out from it destroying the witch and her empire.

The moment everything was over, they meet Ujjwal and other kids too.

Hey, thank you but how did you do that asked Ujjwal.

Three of them looked at each other and smiled

Why are you smiling and what is this ring in your hand Naina?

The golden bell had vanished but the ring of the bell stood with Naina as a ring of gold in her finger. She took that out and swirled in the air only to make them get back into their hotel rooms within their respective beds.

When kids opened their eyes they saw all of their teachers laughing and gossiping as if this episode had never happened but in their heart they knew that they had saved their best friend and the goodness in this world.

Ujjwal realized that Naina is his good friend and thank her for saving her life while apologizing for his banter deeds with her. They both shake hands and promised no fights in the future.

As they reached back, Utsav as usual noted this incident too in his diary and sent his diary to his grandfather as promised. Soon all of them were separated as their father working in Army was posted to another place. However, the lessons of all the love and incidents they all had enjoyed together remained with them. Utsav realized as he was growing up that he had to focus in his studies more, though he kept casual friendship with Naveli and Arushi. Soon his grandfather got his diary edited from professional and sent a book to him which was very famous between youngsters. The grandfather wrote a note too which said "Keep your thoughts positive as someone is listening to you"

Naina realized that fear is nothing but state of mind and her best friend is Miranda. She does not have to search for best friends out there.

Sankalp too overcame his fear of dogs and became courageous.

Rohan and Manas learnt how important it is for them to eat healthy food prepared at home. Manas also started exercising to keep his brain more active and alert.

Vikram stopped showing off as he realized that by showing off he would only make enemies not friends

Ujjwal learnt many lessons out of many and he started practicing OM first thing in the morning which kept him calm and made him very positive and loving in his approach to every situation and humans.

All of them remembered the golden words of Saint whom they had met in jungle "your focus of what is wrong will show you only wrong and your focus on good will show you good" And with this mantra they never failed in any subject and learning the most difficult subject became easy for them.

Images sources

http://pixabay.com/en/seniors-grandparents-couple-walking-311186/

http://pixabay.com/en/cake-birthday-candles-celebration-311791/

http://pixabay.com/en/excited-trip-summer-vacation-23789/

http://pixabay.com/en/girls-ms-sea-bulgaria-seagull-583917/

http://pixabay.com/en/puppy-leash-leashed-jumping-collar-32025/

http://pixabay.com/en/barn-cabin-cottage-autumn-158263/

http://pixabay.com/en/soldier-uniform-army-weapon-60707/

http://pixabay.com/en/pet-pets-girl-dog-puppy-running-312041/

http://pixabay.com/en/mushroom-house-winter-forest-434100/

http://pixabay.com/en/halloween-the-witch-hexenbesen-cat-478582/